Original title:
Sea of Thoughts

Copyright © 2024 Swan Charm
All rights reserved.

Author: Kaido Väinamäe
ISBN HARDBACK: 978-9908-1-2569-5
ISBN PAPERBACK: 978-9908-1-2570-1
ISBN EBOOK: 978-9908-1-2571-8

Echoes Beneath the Surface

Whispers drift on quiet streams,
Unseen tales of life's sweet dreams.
Dancing shadows, flicker light,
Hopes reside in the still night.

Bubbles rise with secrets old,
Stories in the depths unfold.
Life's reflections, soft and clear,
Echoes linger, drawing near.

Distant Horizons of the Heart

Across the sky, a yearning glow,
Paths unseen, where wild winds blow.
Glimmers of hope in twilight's embrace,
Chasing clouds, we find our place.

In the distance, dreams collide,
Bridging gaps where love can hide.
Every heartbeat echoes far,
Guiding us like a shining star.

Fleeting Ripples of Introspection

Thoughts like ripples dance and sway,
In the pond where stillness lay.
Moments brief, yet profound too,
Find the depths that guide you through.

Questions linger, answers tease,
In the quiet, find your peace.
Fleeting thoughts, like shadows glide,
Illuminating truth inside.

Beneath the Calm Waters

Silent depths where dreams reside,
Cradled softly, time's slow tide.
Beneath the surface, life unfolds,
Secrets whisper, stories told.

Gentle currents, soothing sway,
Guide our souls along the way.
In the stillness, hearts align,
Finding solace, pure and fine.

Marooned in Memories

In the quiet of the night,
Old whispers dance and flit,
Lost treasures of the past,
In shadows they still sit.

A cracked frame holds our smiles,
Dust collects on time's embrace,
The laughter slowly fades,
Yet still, I find your trace.

The photographs are faded,
Yet colors still remain,
Each memory like a song,
A bittersweet refrain.

I wander through the echoes,
Where sunlight used to play,
In halls of forgotten dreams,
Where silence holds sway.

With every step I ponder,
What was lost and won,
Marooned in thoughts so deep,
Time can't come undone.

The Drift of Desires

On the wind, our wishes sail,
Like leaves upon a stream,
Twisting through the currents,
Chasing after dreams.

Each desire a whispered note,
Carried on the breeze,
Some find peace in pursuit,
Others drift with ease.

Through the night, the stars beckon,
Guiding hearts aflight,
Amidst the darkened canvas,
They shimmer through the night.

Yet dreams can be elusive,
Fading with the dawn,
An echo of a longing,
As light starts to yawn.

In the quiet of the moment,
We gather hopes anew,
Each sigh a secret wish,
In the morning dew.

Surrender to the Swells

Beneath the roaring surf,
The tides embrace their own,
In foamy white exhale,
Whispers of the deep are grown.

With every crashing wave,
The world begins to sway,
A dance of raw emotion,
In salt and spray at play.

I yield to nature's song,
Let the currents take me far,
In surrender, I find strength,
Held close by ocean's star.

The horizon calls my name,
Where earth meets endless seas,
In the swell, I find my heart,
Floating on the breeze.

Let the swells pull me under,
Where shadows softly merge,
In the heart of water's arms,
I feel the ancient surge.

Beneath the Icy Surface

A frozen world resides,
In silence, whispers hold,
Beneath the icy blanket,
Lies a story untold.

Crystals dance in twilight,
Reflections of the past,
Secrets trapped in winter's grip,
Awaiting the thaw at last.

Each flake a fleeting moment,
A memory caught in time,
Shimmering like starlight,
In a realm so sublime.

Yet beneath the chilly shell,
A warmth begins to stir,
Life pulses in the shadows,
With every heartbeat's blur.

When spring's breath starts to linger,
And the ice begins to break,
The world will rise from slumber,
Awakening from ache.

Tethered to the Shore

The anchor holds with quiet grace,
A gentle pull in the vast embrace.
Seagulls cry above the tide,
While secrets linger, deep inside.

This sandy path my feet have worn,
Is shaped by dreams and tales reborn.
The sun dips low in glowing light,
As shadows stretch to meet the night.

Each wave that crashes sings my name,
In melodies both wild and tame.
The ocean whispers all she's seen,
As time moves on, so soft, serene.

I breathe the salt, I taste the air,
Each moment here, a precious prayer.
Tethered still, I find my way,
In rhythms of the ocean's sway.

Waves of Longing

Beneath the moon, the waters churn,
The tides tell tales of hearts that yearn.
Each crest and trough, a lover's sigh,
As dreams set sail, they rise and fly.

A distant ship, a fleeting glance,
In briny depths, I take my chance.
The currents pull, they guide my quest,
In each embrace, I find my rest.

With echoes soft, the sea calls me,
As hidden truths begin to see.
Waves crash and fall, then rise anew,
Like endless hope, forever true.

The shore, a place where memories dwell,
In secret tides, where whispers swell.
Each wave a promise, each swell a plea,
In depths of longing, I'll find the key.

The Ghosts of Tempests Past

In stormy nights, the shadows creep,
With tales of clouds that loom and leap.
Ghostly winds, they howl and wail,
While echoes of the past set sail.

A ship once battered, now awaits,
In silent docks, where stillness states.
The scars of battles etched in time,
Speak softly in the waves' slow rhyme.

Each lightning flash reveals the view,
Of wreckage lost and dreams askew.
Yet in the dark, a flame still glows,
A hope that in the heart still grows.

The past may linger like a ghost,
In every swell, it calls the most.
Yet from the wreckage, strength is born,
As new dawn breaks the endless scorn.

Unfurling the Mind's Sail

In quiet thoughts, the breeze takes flight,
A canvas blank, yet full of light.
I spread my sails across the sky,
To chase the dreams that float nearby.

Each gust ignites a spark within,
A journey starts where I begin.
With every breath, possibilities rise,
Like ships unfurling toward new skies.

The waves of doubt may crash and roar,
But still I sail, I seek, explore.
The compass turns to paths unseen,
In quest of wonders, I feel keen.

The horizon calls, a siren's song,
I chart my course, where I belong.
With every knot, my spirits soar,
To find the shores worth yearning for.

Tidal Whispers

The moon pulls at the sea,
Echoes soft and low.
Whispers in the breeze,
Where only dreamers go.

Sand between my toes,
A rhythm in the night.
Each wave a secret shared,
In the silver light.

Stars above me shine,
A map of distant skies.
Each glow a promise made,
That time gently defies.

The tide swells and falls,
Like laughter in the dark.
Echoes of the heart,
In each gentle arc.

In this vast expanse,
I find my quiet peace.
Tidal whispers linger,
A sweet, soft release.

Currents of Contemplation

Beneath the flowing waves,
Thoughts drift and collide.
Currents weave a tale,
Of dreams once denied.

In the depths I search,
For answers to the past.
The ocean holds my fears,
In its depths so vast.

Light filters through the blue,
A dance of shadow and grace.
Each ripple tells a story,
Of time and of place.

Moments caught like fish,
Slipping through my grasp.
Currents move, relentless,
While I hold my gasp.

In stillness I find strength,
Amidst the flowing stream.
Currents of contemplation,
Guide me through the dream.

The Ocean Within

Deep within my soul,
A tempest does reside.
Waves crash and they roar,
Seeking to confide.

Tides of joy and sorrow,
Merge in endless flow.
An ocean of emotions,
That few ever know.

In the silence I hear,
Voices soft and true.
The pulse of the sea,
Echoes within too.

Each breath like a wave,
Brings calm or a storm.
The ocean within me,
In its natural form.

Embrace the vastness here,
The beauty and the pain.
The ocean within calls,
To dance in the rain.

Fragments on the Surface

A shell upon the shore,
Holds tales of the deep.
Fragments of a journey,
In silence they sleep.

Each grain of sand whispers,
Secrets of the past.
Waves wash over all,
But memories last.

Colors in the sunset,
Blend into the night.
Fragments of a moment,
In fading light.

The ocean breathes with me,
In rhythms soft and slow.
Fragments on the surface,
Of what I used to know.

Every ebb and flow,
Reflects my heart's own strife.
Fragments drifting softly,
In the dance of life.

Ripples of Insight

In the stillness of dawn's light,
Thoughts awaken, taking flight.
Each reflection, like a wave,
Whispers secrets, wise and brave.

Circles widen, visions clear,
Embrace the silence, hold it dear.
In the water's gentle sway,
Truths emerge, come what may.

Subtle hints in every splash,
Moments fleeting, gone in a flash.
Yet in their dance, we find our way,
A guiding path, a brighter day.

Every ripple, every sigh,
Echoes softly, passing by.
In the stillness, let them flow,
Awakening what we long to know.

Chasing the Horizon

Footsteps fall on golden sand,
Waves retreat, at my command.
Chasing dreams as day breaks free,
Horizon calls, it beckons me.

Clouds streak by, painted skies,
A canvas where the spirit flies.
Each heartbeat, racing with desire,
Drawn to places truly higher.

The sun dips low, a fiery glow,
In the chase, the passions grow.
With every mile, I seek the new,
Visions bright in vibrant hue.

Wind whispers tales of lands afar,
Guiding me like a distant star.
No bounds to hold, no chains to bind,
With open heart and fearless mind.

Storms of Serenity

Amidst the chaos, calm resides,
Where inner peace and love abides.
Tempests rage, yet still I stand,
In tranquil heart, I find my land.

Raindrops fall like gentle tears,
Washing away all my fears.
In the storm's embrace, I grow,
Finding strength in ebb and flow.

Lightning cracks, the thunder rolls,
Nature sings of ancient souls.
In the swirl, a dance divine,
Harmony where sorrows intertwine.

As winds may howl, and shadows creep,
In quietude, my spirit leaps.
For in the tempest, I discover,
The calm that wraps, a hidden cover.

The Mind's Tidal Pool

Thoughts pool like water, deep and clear,
Reflections dance, drawing near.
Echoes of wisdom, past and wise,
In stillness, the heart complies.

Waves of clarity gently rise,
Beneath the surface, truth belies.
In the depths, the shadows play,
Fleeting moments, night and day.

Ideas swirl in quiet grace,
Like drifting leaves in a sacred space.
Pulling back and crashing forth,
Emerging tides show my true worth.

In the dance of thought and time,
I find the rhythm, pure and prime.
In the tidal pull, I breathe, I see,
This tidal pool becomes my key.

Sailing to Stillness

Waves whisper secrets soft and low,
The sun dips down with a golden glow.
Sails unfurl like dreams set free,
As the horizon beckons, calling me.

Gentle breezes carry hopes anew,
As stars appear in the evening blue.
With every breath, the world stands still,
In this moment, my heart can fill.

Gliding over waters calm and wide,
Each ripple starts where the soul resides.
In stillness, I find my place to be,
Among the echoes of the sea.

The compass spins, but I'm not lost,
For peace embraces, despite the cost.
Cradled in nature's vast expanse,
I drift away in a timeless dance.

Sifting Through the Sand

Footprints trace journeys on the shore,
Each grain a story, vibrant and raw.
As tides pull back and forth they play,
Whispering tales of the light of day.

With every handful, memories blend,
Childhood laughter, a guardian friend.
Time slips by like shimmering gold,
Revealing treasures yet untold.

Sunlight dances on the waves, so bright,
While shadows linger, fading in night.
Sifting slowly, I find what's true,
In the quiet, I'll gather you.

Winds of change blow softly here,
Carrying hope and also fear.
But as I sift through life's warm sand,
I hold each moment close at hand.

The Ocean's Embrace

The ocean calls with a voice so clear,
A melody sweet that draws me near.
In every wave, a heartbeat flows,
Softly cradling me wherever it goes.

Salt-kissed breeze flows through my skin,
Awakening feelings deep within.
As gulls dance high, I close my eyes,
Beneath the vast and endless skies.

Ebbing tides reveal hidden dreams,
Where sunlight glints and brightly beams.
In this embrace, I find my peace,
A moment where all worries cease.

The rhythm of waves is my song to hum,
A gentle lullaby, a steady drum.
In the ocean's arms, I feel so free,
A union of spirit, the soul and the sea.

Crosscurrents of Thought

In the mind's depths, thoughts intertwine,
Like rivers merging, a delicate line.
Crosscurrents pull in every direction,
Seeking the heart's true connection.

Whispers of dreams clash with fears,
Echoes of laughter, distant tears.
In the chaos, I find my way,
Through the tempest that holds sway.

Moments of clarity spark like light,
Guiding me gently through the night.
With every wave of reflection's tide,
I sort through feelings I cannot hide.

The currents shift, and I must choose,
To navigate paths, win or lose.
But in this dance of heart and mind,
A deeper truth is what I find.

Celestial Castaways

Drifting through the endless night,
Stars whisper secrets, soft and bright.
Lost souls seek a guiding flame,
In the cosmic chess, we play our game.

Comets tailing, silver streaks,
Voices of the past, the present speaks.
In solitude, we find our grace,
The universe, a vast embrace.

Galaxies twirl in silent dance,
Weaving stories, chance by chance.
Amongst the dust, we forge our path,
In the void, we find our wrath.

Once tethered to the earthly ground,
Now floating where no bounds are found.
Castaways in a sea so wide,
In celestial realms, we shall abide.

Each star our friend, each moon our guide,
Upon this endless cosmic ride.
Together lost, together free,
In this vastness, just you and me.

A Voyage Through Dreams

Sailing on the quiet tide,
Where shadows and whispers oft abide.
In realms where wishes softly dwell,
A tapestry of stories we weave so well.

Beneath the moon's gentle gaze,
Dreams unfold in a mystic haze.
With every wave, a memory lost,
For a fleeting dream, we pay the cost.

Uncharted lands behind closed eyes,
Where echoes of laughter gently rise.
Each heartbeat marks a turning page,
In the book of life, we engage.

Winds of wonder beckon near,
In this voyage, we shed all fear.
Through valleys deep, and mountains high,
In the dreamscape, we freely fly.

Awake or asleep, we brave the night,
For in our dreams, we find the light.
Together we drift on this endless stream,
Forever bound in a voyage of dreams.

Distant Shores of Memory

Waves crash softly on golden sand,
Whispers of time, hand in hand.
Distant echoes call my name,
In the heart, they spark a flame.

Each tide brings a story anew,
Faded pictures, a transient view.
Footprints washed away by time,
In the silence, ghosts start to rhyme.

Treasured moments like seashells,
Buried deep where nostalgia dwells.
In the shadows, laughter flows,
A tender song and love that glows.

Across the sea, the heart does soar,
To distant shores and evermore.
Regrets like tides may ebb and wane,
Yet memories linger, sweet yet plain.

With every wave, the past returns,
In the heart, a lantern burns.
On this journey toward the light,
Distant shores guide me through the night.

Under the Surface

Beneath the waves, a world concealed,
Mysteries of the sea revealed.
Where silence reigns and shadows creep,
A realm of secrets, dark and deep.

Coral gardens, vibrant and rare,
Home to creatures beyond compare.
In waters clear, reflections dance,
Life unfolds in a rhythmic trance.

Sunbeams filter through the blue,
Kissing depths where wonders brew.
Glimmers of gold and hues so bright,
In this underwater haven, light.

Yet down below, the echoes call,
Whispers of those who rise and fall.
Memories linger, tales untold,
In silence, the heart grows bold.

Under the surface, fears take flight,
In the stillness, dreams ignite.
Together we'll dive, hand in hand,
In this sacred, submerged land.

The Coral Reef of Reflection

Beneath the blue, a world sublime,
Colors dance in rhythmic time.
Fish glint like gems, weaving through
A tapestry of life, ever new.

Silent whispers of the sea,
Echo secrets, wild and free.
Coral towers, shadows play,
In this realm, we drift away.

Waves carry dreams to distant shores,
Each tide opens ancient doors.
In this maze of deep delight,
We navigate the azure night.

Reflections sparkle in the light,
Guiding souls like stars at night.
In the stillness, thoughts unfold,
A treasure chest of stories told.

With every dive, depths to explore,
Mysteries linger near the shore.
In the coral's gentle glow,
We find the peace that hearts long for.

Wind in the Mind's Sails

Gentle breezes stir the thought,
Ideas soaring, battles fought.
Sails unfurl, the canvas bright,
Navigating through day and night.

The whispers carry tales of old,
Of dreams pursued and hearts bold.
In the mind, the currents flow,
Charting paths, we learn to grow.

Thoughts like clouds drift far and wide,
With every gust, they swell with pride.
Chasing horizons, chasing fate,
With every breath, we illuminate.

When the storms of doubt arise,
Hold steadfast, reach for the skies.
For in the tempest, truths reveal,
The strength within, the heart can feel.

Onward, onward, let dreams prevail,
Adventures await, with wind in our sail.
The journey's essence, wild and free,
In the mind's embrace, eternity.

Charting Uncharted Waters

Beyond the maps, where few have tread,
Lies a landscape, full of dread.
Yet in the unknown, wonders gleam,
A canvas vast, time's greatest dream.

The horizon whispers, soft and clear,
"Venture forth, cast away fear."
Each ripple holds a tale untold,
In azure depths, brave stories unfold.

Stars above guide the way anew,
With every gust, horizons grew.
On this journey, spirits entwine,
In uncharted realms, hearts align.

New shores beckon, courage ignite,
With dreams like anchors, futures bright.
Though waters challenge, we embrace,
In each wave, we find our place.

Charting paths with hearts ablaze,
Through unknown seas, we set our gaze.
For every storm gives way to light,
In the uncharted, we find our flight.

The Horizon's Embrace

Where land meets sky in soft embrace,
A meeting point, time finds its grace.
Golden hues blend warmth and blue,
In this haven, dreams renew.

Beyond the waves, the future glows,
In every sunrise, promise flows.
Chasing shadows, letting go,
In the horizon's arms, we grow.

Each step forward, hearts in sync,
Awash in colors, we pause and think.
For in the distance, glimpses call,
A place of hope where we won't fall.

As sunsets blend in fiery delight,
Stars emerge to claim the night.
With every breath, we weave a tale,
In the horizon's embrace, we sail.

The journey stretches, ever wide,
In the arms of dreams, we confide.
And as the day meets twilight's grace,
We find our peace in the horizon's embrace.

Navigating Inner Depths

In shadows deep, where silence dwells,
I chart my course through echoing spells.
Thoughts like phantoms, they drift and weave,
In the depths of the heart, I strive to believe.

Waves of doubt crash on the shore,
Fears grow restless, seeking more.
Yet in the murmur, a whisper glows,
Guiding my spirit where the truth flows.

I dive beneath the surface bright,
Into the realm of the hidden light.
Treasures await in the darkest sea,
Unlocking the chains that once bound me.

With courage as my steady sail,
I voyage where others might fail.
Each stroke reveals the depths I own,
In these waters, I am not alone.

So I navigate with heart and mind,
Unraveling threads, the fabric entwined.
Through the inner depths, I shall glide,
To find the peace that longs to reside.

Islands of Introspection

Upon the shores of quiet thought,
I wander where my mind is caught.
Islands rise from the sea of grey,
Offering solace in their stay.

Each grain of sand, a moment passed,
Reflections of shadows that last.
I build castles with introspection,
Crafting dreams with sweet connection.

The winds of change whisper my name,
As tides of feeling rise like flame.
I stroll the beaches, lost in mind,
To seek the treasures that I find.

Beneath the palms, my spirit rests,
In this haven, I feel truly blessed.
With every wave, I shed a tear,
For memories dear that linger near.

So I embrace these islands true,
Each thought and feeling, old and new.
In introspection, I find my way,
On these shores, I long to stay.

Whirlpools of Wonder

In the whirlpools of wonder, I dive so deep,
Where dreams and realities quietly creep.
Spiraling thoughts in a dance divine,
Lost for a moment, yet perfectly fine.

Colors collide in a vibrant swirl,
Ideas bounce forth, like seashells they twirl.
Time dissolves in these currents bright,
Each pulse of creation unveils a new light.

I grasp at the edges of chaos and calm,
Finding treasures hidden beneath the balm.
As I swirl with the magic of what could be,
Every turn whispers secrets to me.

In this maelstrom of thought and delight,
I lose myself, but I find my sight.
For wonder ignites a fire within,
A passion awakened for life to begin.

Through these whirlpools, I gracefully flow,
Unraveling mysteries, letting them grow.
In the dance of wonder, I choose to stay,
For each moment is precious, come what may.

The Currents of Memory

In currents of memory, time drifts away,
Floating on whispers of yesterday.
Images shimmer like stars in the night,
Guiding my heart with their fragile light.

Echoes of laughter, shadows of tears,
Riding the waves of the passing years.
Each moment that passes, a story unfolds,
In the river of life, our truth is told.

I gather the fragments, both tender and bright,
Weaving them softly into the night.
As currents rush forward, I hold the past dear,
For the sails of tomorrow are built from here.

The tides of our lives ebb and flow,
Carrying dreams where memories glow.
In this vast ocean, I cast my net wide,
To catch every memory that waits to abide.

So I sail on these currents, my heart open wide,
Honoring moments that time cannot hide.
In the flow of existence, I find my own way,
Navigating the waters where memories play.

Nautical Notions

Sails unfurl in the gentle breeze,
Whispers of the sea call us with ease.
Waves dance lightly, a rhythmic song,
Guiding the heart where we belong.

Stars above twinkle, a vast delight,
Mapping our course through the quiet night.
Echoes of laughter, the crew so bold,
Adventures await as the tales unfold.

The horizon stretches, endless and wide,
Beneath the sun, on the ocean's tide.
Each splash of water sings of the past,
In nautical dreams, our spirits are cast.

Anchors away, let our worries cease,
Sailing on journeys that bring us peace.
With every wave, a new path to chart,
Nautical notions, a sailor's heart.

Tempest of Ideas

In the storm of thought, ideas collide,
Whirling like leaves in the fierce winds' stride.
Lightning flashes, illuminating night,
Sparks of brilliance, a fierce delight.

Thunder rolls like the heart's own beat,
Thoughts resound, refusing defeat.
In chaos lies the seeds of creation,
Tempestuous winds bring new foundation.

Waves of emotion crash on the shore,
Each surging wave brings forth something more.
In tempests wild, we find our true voice,
For in the turmoil, we make our choice.

Ideas like rain pour down from the skies,
Washing away all the mundane lies.
Through the turmoil, we rise and we grow,
In every tempest, new visions flow.

Under the Starry Skies

Beneath the cloak of night so deep,
Whispers of dreams begin to seep.
Stars above twinkle in soft array,
Guiding our hearts as we drift away.

The moon casts silver on the lake,
Ripples shimmer with every shake.
A canvas painted with cosmic light,
Under the heavens, we take flight.

Gentle breezes softly sway,
Carrying wishes that drift and play.
In the stillness, our thoughts align,
Under the stars, your hand in mine.

Constellations tell stories of old,
Of lovers and dreamers, of brave and bold.
In this magic, our spirits ascend,
Under the starry skies, we transcend.

Serene Waters of Wonder

Crystal clear waters, a tranquil hue,
Reflecting the sky, every shade and cue.
Ripples dance gently, a soft embrace,
Serene waters holding a sacred space.

Nature's whisper flows through the air,
Every heartbeat, a promise to care.
In this stillness, we find our peace,
From life's chaos, a sweet release.

The horizon beckons with beauty profound,
In the depths of the water, treasures abound.
Each moment a pearl, so rare and bright,
Serene waters cradle our souls in light.

As sunsets blend with the night's cool grace,
Stars begin glimmering, finding their place.
In the silence, a world to discover,
Serene waters of wonder, our hearts hover.

Nautical Dreams

In the hush of dawn's soft light,
Sails unfurl, the sea's delight.
Whispers of waves, a gentle call,
To distant lands where dreams enthrall.

Stars above, a guiding glow,
Through currents deep, where fantasies flow.
The horizon sings a siren's tune,
Beneath the watchful, silver moon.

Adventures wait in the oceans wide,
With each heartbeat, the tides confide.
Mysteries dance on the ocean's crest,
In nautical dreams, we find our rest.

Seagulls cry as they gracefully soar,
Every moment, we yearn for more.
The limitless blue, our hearts embrace,
In this vast realm, we find our place.

So let us sail, let spirits rise,
In a world where freedom lies.
With dreams as compass, we'll navigate,
The oceans of time, where we create.

Beyond the Shallows

Where the waters meet the light,
Secrets lurk, just out of sight.
In the depths, a silent song,
Whispering truths that feel so strong.

Coral gardens, colors bloom,
Hidden realms dispel the gloom.
With every breath, the world expands,
Beyond the shallows, love demands.

In the quiet, treasures wait,
A dance of fate, we captivate.
The ocean's pulse, a steady beat,
Pulls us closer, with each heartbeat.

Journey bold, away we glide,
With courage as our only guide.
Through azure waves, we seek and find,
A deeper love, a boundless mind.

So dive beneath the tranquil tide,
Where dreams await, and fears subside.
Beyond the shallows, we'll explore,
The depths of life, forevermore.

Storms and Serenity

Dark clouds gather, the winds collide,
Nature's fury, we cannot hide.
Lightning strikes, a violent dance,
In chaos, we must take our chance.

Yet within the tempest's roar,
Comes a whisper, a distant shore.
Beneath the rage, a calm resides,
In the eye of storms, where peace abides.

As thunder rumbles, hearts awake,
In every shatter, the bonds we make.
Together lost, yet found anew,
In storms and serenity, we break through.

The tides may turn, the skies may weep,
But in our souls, the promise deep.
After the storm, the skies grow clear,
With every challenge, we persevere.

So let the winds howl, let the waves rise,
For in this journey, we grow wise.
Through storms and grace, we find our way,
Embracing night, embracing day.

Uncharted Territories of Emotion

In the labyrinth of the heart,
Where shadows dwell and dreams depart.
Each feeling maps an unknown land,
A journey vast, yet carefully planned.

Waves of joy crash on the shore,
Sorrow mingles, seeking more.
With every pulse, we navigate,
Uncharted territories we create.

In laughter's echo, the skies ignite,
With whispered love, we take flight.
Through valleys low and peaks so high,
In this expanse, we learn to fly.

Fear may whisper, doubt may creep,
Yet in our truth, the heart's a leap.
Boldly we tread on shifting sands,
Exploring worlds with open hands.

So come, let's traverse this sacred space,
With every heartbeat, we embrace.
In these uncharted realms, we find,
The depth of love that knows no bind.

The Submerged Soul

In depths where shadows linger,
A heart beats, silent vow.
Beneath the weight of water,
The soul drifts, seeking how.

Lost whispers of the twilight,
Echo in the waking haze.
An anchor tied to memories,
Yet dreams cut through the maze.

With each wave, a tale unfolds,
Of love that time forgot.
Fragments float like drifting leaves,
In currents fiercely caught.

A sunbeam pierces slowly,
Awakening the night.
In quiet depths, the journey,
Is the path toward the light.

So let the tides carry forth,
The remnants of the past.
For in the depths, the spirit glows,
A find that holds steadfast.

Flotsam of Fantasies

Upon the ocean's surface,
Dreams gather, wild and free.
Like shards of glass that sparkle,
In gentle symphony.

Each thought a wave, drifting far,
Carried by unseen hands.
A flotilla of wishes,
Adrift on starry sands.

In the night, whispers linger,
Borne on tides of the mind.
Fleeting glimpses of our hopes,
In the vastness, we find.

As the moonlight fades softly,
A glimmer leads us home.
Navigating through the darkness,
In the dreams that we roam.

Let the ocean hold our fears,
Transform them into tides.
For in the sea of fancies,
Our true self abides.

Surfacing Ideas

From depths of silent pondering,
Bright thoughts emerge anew.
Like bubbles bursting in sunlight,
They rise, a vibrant hue.

Ideas dance on waters,
In patterns never drawn.
They shimmer in the morning,
Greeting the edge of dawn.

With each crest of inspiration,
A wave of clarity forms.
In the swirl of perception,
Creativity warms.

Let the currents guide the vision,
As muses flicker near.
With every rise and fall, we learn,
To flow through doubt and fear.

So plunge into the depths,
Where wisdom waits to breathe.
Surfacing bright ideas,
The heart of life beneath.

Beneath the Waves of Worry

In shadows where the secrets lie,
A tempest brews within.
The ocean's roar, a harbinger,
Of quiet battles fought in.

Waves crash like anxious pulses,
Restless in their flight.
Yet stillness hides a refuge,
Beneath the frothy light.

Thoughts swirl like whirlpools,
In ever-turbulent seas.
The weight of all our burdens,
Becomes the gentle breeze.

But in the lull between the storms,
A calmness softly waits.
Reminding us that after fear,
The sun still radiates.

So dive beneath those worries,
And find the peace below.
For in the depths of stillness,
True strength begins to grow.

Flotsam of the Soul

Drifting whispers in the tide,
Fragments hidden far and wide,
Bottled dreams that ebb and flow,
Lost treasures from long ago.

Echoes soft on winds that sigh,
Matters deep, we can't deny,
Waves will rise and fall in turn,
Lessons taught, we still must learn.

Shadowed thoughts on velvet seas,
Sand and salt with every breeze,
Carried forth by fate's embrace,
Reflections of a hidden place.

Beneath the surf, a heart will beat,
Silent calls we must repeat,
Rescue from the darkened swell,
Flotsam conjures tales to tell.

Sailing Through the Unknown

Open sails to skies so vast,
Drifting toward horizons past,
Stars will guide the path ahead,
Dreams await where fears have tread.

An unseen compass shows the way,
In shadows where the truth may sway,
Whispers of the ocean's lore,
Unwritten tales on distant shore.

Through tempests fierce and waters deep,
We sail on, our promises to keep,
Every wave a song we sing,
In the heart, the wanderlust ring.

Charting courses bold and bright,
Embracing both the day and night,
Each horizon holds its grace,
Sailing forth into time and space.

The Abyssal Mindscape

Underneath the surface deep,
In shadowed realms, our secrets keep,
Thoughts like fish that dart and hide,
In the depths, where fears abide.

A world unknown awaits the brave,
In currents strong, our hearts must wave,
Visions swirl in darkened seas,
Tangled webs of memories.

The silent echoes call our names,
Dancing flames of quiet games,
Consciousness a drifting boat,
Clinging to each fleeting note.

With every dive, the shadows sway,
Leading us on paths astray,
Wisdom found beneath the veil,
In the abyss, we shall sail.

Churning Sands of Contemplation

Time's grains shifting in the breeze,
Thoughts like shadows dance with ease,
Footprints left upon the shore,
Questions linger evermore.

Beneath the sun's relentless gaze,
We ponder life in winding ways,
Each gust carries tales untold,
Secrets ages have enfolded.

In the stillness, echoes grow,
Forming paths through winds that blow,
Every grain a story shared,
Memories of hearts that dared.

Constructing castles in the sand,
Built on dreams we dare to stand,
Fleeting thoughts like whispers fall,
In churning sands, they beckon all.

Tidepools of Reflection

In shallow waters, secrets hide,
Crabs dance gently, a tide's soft glide.
Shells whisper tales of distant shores,
Echoes of waves, where time implores.

Sunlight flutters, a golden crest,
Each ripple sings of nature's best.
Bubbles rise with dreams untold,
A world beneath, both shy and bold.

Waves retreat to reveal the past,
Silent stories, in shadows cast.
Finding treasures, lost and new,
In tidepools deep, where thoughts break through.

Glimmers of hope in seaweed green,
Moments cherished, softly seen.
Every glance, a fleeting chance,
In nature's arms, we sway and dance.

As night descends, the stars ignite,
Tidepools reflect their shimmering light.
With every wave, we find our way,
In liquid dreams, we long to stay.

Floating Thoughts

Drifting gently on the breeze,
Thoughts like feathers, light and free.
In whispers soft, they swirl and twirl,
Carried away, like a ribboned pearl.

Clouds above weave tales of old,
Stories of moments yet untold.
Letting go is the sweetest art,
As dreams take flight, they mend the heart.

Sailing on the streams of time,
A symphony of thoughts in rhyme.
Each note a color, bright and bold,
In the heart's canvas, they unfold.

Colors merge in a cosmic blend,
Floating on whispers, around the bend.
Like whispers on the morning air,
Each thought a journey that we share.

In stillness found, we drift and sway,
Floating thoughts lead the way.
In the quiet, the mind's embrace,
We find our home, our sacred space.

Compass of Wanderlust

With open heart, I chase the dawn,
The world awaits, reborn, withdrawn.
Paths unknown, like veins they weave,
A compass draws where I believe.

Mountains rise, their peaks in snow,
Rivers whisper, where dreams can flow.
Each footstep echoes, a tale unspun,
In lands afar, my heart is won.

Stars above guide restless eyes,
Under the vast, cerulean skies.
The map unfolds, horizons gleam,
Every destination, a shared dream.

Through forests deep and deserts wide,
Endless wonders on this ride.
In every sunset, colors twist,
A call to venture, a wanderer's tryst.

Home is where the heart takes flight,
In every journey, day and night.
With compass set, my spirit roams,
In this vast world, I find my home.

Beneath the Unseen

In shadows cast, beneath the light,
Mysteries linger, out of sight.
Beneath the surface, whispers dwell,
Untold stories, a silent spell.

The heartbeats echo, soft and low,
In hidden depths where feelings flow.
A tapestry woven from dreams and fears,
In the quiet corners, love appears.

Threads of gold entwine the dark,
Glimmers of hope, a tiny spark.
Within the silence, a rhythmic dance,
Beneath the unseen, we take our chance.

Roots reach down, where secrets lie,
In the soil rich, where spirits sigh.
Every glance, a fleeting chance,
To discover the depth of our expanse.

With open hearts, we plumb the soul,
Unraveling truths that make us whole.
Beneath the unseen, we find our way,
In the shadows, love holds sway.

Harbor of Hopes

In the stillness of the night,
Whispers ride the gentle breeze.
Stars like dreams take their flight,
Guiding hearts towards ease.

Boats sway softly at the dock,
Promises linger in the air.
Each wave a silent clock,
Time holds secrets we all share.

Lanterns flicker, casting light,
Shadows dance upon the ground.
In this place, all fears take flight,
And lost souls can be found.

The horizon calls with its glow,
Endless journeys yet to start.
In this harbor, we all know,
Hope is safe within the heart.

As dawn breaks with hues so bright,
A new day dawns, fresh and clear.
In the harbor, dreams take flight,
Carrying all we hold dear.

Fishing for Clarity

Cast the line into the deep,
Waiting for the tug of fate.
Thoughts swirl like the waters sweep,
Hopes and fears negotiate.

The bobber dances on the tide,
Waiting for a fish to bite.
In this stillness, secrets hide,
Trying to find what feels right.

Ripples break the perfect calm,
Questions rise, the answers swirl.
Nature whispers a subtle balm,
Guiding hearts through life's great whirl.

With patience comes the hopeful catch,
Revealed in silent, sacred space.
Each moment teaches us to match,
Wonders met with gentle grace.

The net comes full, yet still we yearn,
For clarity in every cast.
In this journey, there's much to learn,
And every day can be our last.

Lighthouse of Longing

Standing tall against the storm,
Its beam cuts through the night.
A sentinel, faithfully warm,
Guiding lost souls towards light.

Waves crash against the rocky shore,
Whispers of dreams yet untold.
In its shadow, longing soars,
Each heart carries a wish bold.

The light swings wide, a beacon strong,
Calling sailors to their fate.
In the silence, one can belong,
Embracing love as they wait.

Darkness fades with each new glow,
Hope ignites like a flare.
Distance shrinks as feelings grow,
In this haven, truth lays bare.

The lighthouse stands through night and day,
A steadfast friend when skies are grey.
In every beam, we find our way,
Longings met without delay.

Drifting With Discontent

On a raft of tangled dreams,
Drifting where the shadows fall.
The current pulls at silent seams,
A whispered ache within us all.

Clouds gather heavy in the sky,
Each gust a sigh upon the breeze.
Questions rise when hopes run dry,
Searching still for inner peace.

Drifting far from what is known,
In waves of doubt, we feel afloat.
Everything changes, nothing's grown,
Silent hearts begin to gloat.

Yet still we float on troubled seas,
Caught between what is and was.
In the stillness, a gentle tease,
Of finding joy in what was lost.

As the moon glares down in wrath,
Reflections cast upon the sea.
Each sway of fate, we choose our path,
In discontent, we're truly free.

Saltwater Soliloquy

Waves whisper secrets of the deep,
Carried on breezes, their promises sweep.
Salt on my lips, the ocean's embrace,
Each tide a reminder, a timeless space.

Crabs scuttle past, in dance with the sand,
Footprints washed away, lost in the strand.
Seagulls cry out, their call fills the air,
Nature's raw beauty, a moment to share.

Clouds drift like dreams, over water they glide,
Beneath the vast sky, my worries subside.
The sun sets ablaze, painting warmth on the sea,
In this sacred stillness, I find my heart free.

Drifting in thought, with each passing wave,
The rhythm of life, both gentle and brave.
Saltwater whispers, they echo my soul,
In this liquid world, I feel truly whole.

Abyss of Ambivalence

In the depth of the sea, emotions collide,
A dance of the heart, where shadows reside.
Waves roll like choices, a constant debate,
Torn between currents that twist and sedate.

With each ebb and flow, I question my path,
A tug-of-war pulling, provoking the wrath.
What lies beneath? A treasure or bane?
In this swirling abyss, I struggle with pain.

Silence a beacon, amidst all the noise,
In seeking the truth, I must find my voice.
Doubt tugs at my sleeve, like kelp in the tide,
Yet hope rises harshly, like light in the wide.

A storm brews inside, tempest hard to chart,
Questions like waves, crashing hard on my heart.
Yet through the chaos, I sense something pure,
A glimmer of clarity, my thoughts to assure.

Navigating the depths, through shadows I flee,
Courage the compass, to set my heart free.
In the abyss of ambivalence, I'll learn to be whole,
Emerging from darkness, renewed in my soul.

Nautical Notions

Sails billow open, dreams catch the breeze,
The horizon beckons, with whispers of seas.
Stars guide the way, through each darkened night,
Charting the course, where hopes take flight.

Anchors of memories, weigh heavy my heart,
Each port a chapter, where journeys depart.
On waves of adventure, I carve out my song,
With nautical notions, where I feel I belong.

The compass spins wildly, as passions collide,
From tranquil lagoons to the storms that divide.
Gold grains of sunset, on water they lay,
A tapestry woven, of night into day.

Fishermen's laughter, tales shared with the tide,
The ocean's a mirror, where secrets confide.
Seashells are treasures, with stories untold,
In the vastness of blue, I lose and unfold.

Steering through waters, both calm and uncouth,
I sail with my spirit, in quest of the truth.
Nautical notions, they guide me along,
In the symphony of waves, I find where I'm strong.

Echoes of Silence

In stillness I wander, where whispers are loud,
Among the quiet, where thoughts are unbowed.
Echoes of silence, in shadows they creep,
A sanctuary found, in moments so deep.

Stars blink above, like secrets they keep,
The world holds its breath, as the night starts to seep.
Time pauses briefly, as shadows converge,
In this tender moment, emotions emerge.

Breath of the night, cool against my skin,
A refuge in darkness, where feelings begin.
Listening closely, to the hum of the year,
Echoes of silence, whispering near.

The heart knows its rhythm, a pulse in the void,
In silence profound, all chaos destroyed.
Thoughts drift like clouds, so heavy yet light,
In the realm of the quiet, I find my true sight.

So here I will linger, in the still of the night,
Finding my voice, in the absence of fright.
Echoes of silence will guide me back home,
In this tranquil space, I shall learn to roam.

Castaways of Memory

Drifting on the tides of time,
Whispers of the past collide.
Faded echoes softly chime,
In the heart where dreams reside.

Lost in the sands of memories,
Fragments scattered, tales untold.
Searching through the histories,
For treasures of the heart to hold.

Veils of laughter, tears like rain,
Each moment crafted, bittersweet.
In the labyrinth of the brain,
We find the paths where lovers meet.

Ghostly shadows dance and play,
In the corridors of our mind.
They remind us of yesterday,
What we cherish, what we find.

Yet through the fog, we brightly shine,
With the light of lessons learned.
For in our hearts, we intertwine,
In the flame, the memory burned.

Fluid Fragments

Waves of thought begin to flow,
Drifting through the seams of night.
Memories in currents glow,
Shadows dancing, soft and light.

Fragments shift like sand and sea,
Reflections of a hidden dream.
Each glimpse a part of me,
Caught within the fleeting stream.

Time unveils its gentle brush,
Painting stories, bold yet pure.
In the silence, moments hush,
Leaving traces to endure.

Liquid echoes, fleeting grace,
Fleeting thoughts in endless flight.
They hold the past in soft embrace,
Nestled deep within the night.

Finding peace within the flow,
Resilience in each rising tide.
In these fragments, we all grow,
As the heart learns to abide.

The Horizon's Embrace

Where the sky and waters meet,
Dreams unfold and hopes arise.
In the light, our souls are sweet,
Bathed in warmth of endless skies.

Every wave a whispered prayer,
Carried on the breath of breeze.
Longing hearts in stillness share,
Secrets held between the trees.

Watching colors blend and merge,
As daylight fades to twilight's hue.
In the moment, spirits surge,
A vow between the old and new.

Embracing all that is unknown,
With courage as our guiding star.
In the vastness, we have grown,
No matter where we wander far.

Through the distance, visions call,
Promising a brighter place.
Together, we shall never fall,
In the horizon's warm embrace.

Navigating Thoughtful Waters

Through the currents of our mind,
We sail on ships of dreams and fears.
Gently, thoughts begin to unwind,
Catching whispers, shedding tears.

Charts of hope, the stars our guide,
In the night we find our way.
With each wave, emotions glide,
Tales of joy and sorrow play.

Companions on this vast expanse,
We share our burdens, light the load.
In the dance of chance and chance,
Together, we shall forge the road.

Every storm that rages fierce,
Teaches us to stand up tall.
Through the trials, hearts may pierce,
But we shall rise, we shall not fall.

Navigating thoughtful streams,
Finding peace in gentle flows.
In our hearts, we'll keep the dreams,
As the river of life grows.

Sheltered by Waves

In the cradle of the sea, they sway,
Whispers of salt and spray.
Beneath the moon's soft gaze,
The world in rhythm plays.

Bubbles rise with tales untold,
Secrets of the deep they hold.
Embraced by tides, so free,
I drift in harmony.

The sun dips low, a fiery hue,
Burnishing waves in golden view.
In this sanctuary, I find,
Peaceful moments intertwined.

Shells crunch softly beneath my feet,
Each treasure found, a heartbeat.
Nature's song, a soothing balm,
In sea's embrace, I am calm.

Time flows like the gentle tide,
Endless journey, no need to hide.
Sheltered here, my spirit roams,
With the waves, I build my homes.

Lingering on the Shore

Footprints fade with the tide's song,
Waves that come and go along.
The horizon, a distant call,
I linger here, enthralled by it all.

Seagulls dance in the salty air,
Wings outstretched without a care.
Each gust of wind a friendly hand,
Guiding dreams upon the sand.

Time slips softly like grains of sand,
Reflections drift upon the strand.
In twilight's glow, I find my place,
Beneath the sky's warm embrace.

The sun departs, the stars ignite,
A canvas painted in the night.
I breathe in deep, the ocean's air,
Knowing here, my heart lays bare.

Lingering moments weave a tale,
In each breath of wind that sails.
Eternity in whispers shared,
Among the waves, my spirit bared.

Nautical Musings

Beneath the vast and endless blue,
Whispers of the ocean brew.
Thoughts like ships begin to roam,
Seeking solace, finding home.

Stars above, a guiding light,
Navigating through the night.
In the silence, I can hear,
Echoes of what brought me here.

Tales of sailors long ago,
Adventures far where few would go.
Every wave a voice, a song,
In the currents, I belong.

Crafting dreams on paper tides,
With the breeze, my heart abides.
The canvas broad, the ink of seas,
Each stroke captured in the breeze.

Nautical musings take their flight,
Guiding me through day and night.
With every swell, I find my muse,
In ocean's heart, I cannot lose.

Castaway Contemplations

On distant shores where silence reigns,
A lonely heart reflects the pains.
Castaway dreams, lost and found,
In each grain of sand, they abound.

Driftwood whispers tales of strife,
Echoing the remnants of life.
Beneath the moon's watchful eye,
I ponder, question, wonder why.

The ocean breathes, a rhythmic sigh,
Every wave a lullaby.
In solitude, I weave my thoughts,
Transforming sorrow into knots.

Paths untaken, choices made,
In twilight's glow, the fears I'm laid.
Nature's brush paints skies of gray,
Yet in the storm, I'll find my way.

With every dawn, rebirth begins,
A castaway's journey slowly spins.
In contemplation, strength I find,
A treasure hidden deep in mind.

Waves of Whimsy

Whispers dance upon the shore,
Colors bright, forevermore.
Frolicsome in splashes bold,
Stories of old, yet untold.

Shells and treasures found at sea,
Each a glimpse of reverie.
Laughter echoes in the breeze,
Carried far with playful ease.

Kites soar high beneath the sun,
Chasing dreams, we're all in fun.
In the tide, we shed our cares,
Joyful hearts, free as air.

Gentle waves that kiss the sand,
Nature's art, a perfect hand.
Where the sea meets sky's embrace,
Life's a dance, a merry race.

In this realm of playful light,
Magic glimmers, pure delight.
The ocean's song, forever sung,
Where youth and wisdom are still young.

Currents of Reflection

Mirror of the tranquil stream,
Where thoughts drift and softly gleam.
Ripples form with every sigh,
Memories float, then whisper by.

Silent nights beneath the stars,
Pondering love, life's many scars.
In the depths, our truths collide,
Echoes of the heart abide.

Moments captured, fleeting, sweet,
Every heartbeat, bittersweet.
In the flow, we find our way,
Guided gently, night and day.

Reflections dance on water's face,
Waves of time that leave no trace.
Each thought a compass, a guide,
Navigating the ebbing tide.

As the currents gently fade,
We embrace the life we've made.
In solitude, we come to see,
Within the depths, we find the key.

Tides of the Mind

Thoughts that ebb and flow like seas,
Caught in currents, a gentle breeze.
High and low, they rise and fall,
A never-ending, silent call.

Ideas wash upon the shore,
Crafting visions, opening doors.
In the chaos, wisdom gleams,
Reflecting on our silent dreams.

Waves of doubt may crash and break,
Yet from the foam, new paths we make.
In every tide, a chance to grow,
Through stormy nights, we start to know.

As the oceans stretch so wide,
With every turn, we learn to glide.
In whispers soft, the tides confide,
Revealing truths that we can't hide.

Let the mind be open seas,
Trust the flow, and seek the keys.
In the tides, we find our way,
Through thoughts that dance, bold and sway.

Driftwood Dreams

Worn by waves and time's embrace,
Driftwood telling tales of grace.
Each knot and twist, a story shares,
Life lived bold, beyond repairs.

From far-off shores, they journeyed here,
Silent whispers, hearts sincere.
In every grain, a world is seen,
Dreams of sea, wild and serene.

Nestled on the sandy bed,
Ancient paths where few have tread.
Lost wanderers, eternally,
Seek the peace of memory.

With every swell, a secret hides,
Amongst the tides, where magic bides.
Join the dance of dreams afloat,
In the breeze, our hopes can coat.

So gather 'round this circle wide,
Where driftwood dreams and hearts collide.
In the twilight, stories gleam,
Reality bends into a dream.

Wash of Wistfulness

The waves whisper softly at night,
Memories linger like soft moonlight.
Each tide carries echoes of dreams,
In quiet reflection, nothing's as it seems.

Granules of sand slip from my hand,
Moments once cherished, now drift like land.
The ocean's sigh speaks of what was,
A gentle reminder, a lingering cause.

Footprints erased by the cool sea breeze,
Hearts once tethered now drift with ease.
In the wash of emotions, we begin to float,
Drifting apart on a small, sturdy boat.

Yet in the distance, the horizon gleams,
A flicker of hope, in the weave of dreams.
The tides may shift, and the heart may sway,
But in misty memories, we find our way.

Between the Tides

The sea pulls back, revealing the shore,
Secrets hidden, waiting to explore.
Whispers of salt on a sunlit day,
Promises forgotten, washed far away.

Footsteps by the water, a tender trace,
Each moment lost in time's fierce race.
Ebb flows gently, a quiet reprieve,
Between the tides, it's hard to believe.

Shells and stones tell stories of years,
Captured laughter, forgotten tears.
Meeting the surface, an ebbing embrace,
Between the tides, we hold our place.

To ride the waves of our dreams anew,
As stars twinkle bright in the ocean's blue.
The journey continues, onward we stride,
Navigating life, between every tide.

Ebb and Flow of Feelings

A heartbeat dances with the moon's glow,
Like the ocean's rhythm, it ebbs and flows.
Moments of stillness, whispers of grace,
Captured in silence, we find our place.

Waves crash softly on the weathered rocks,
Bringing with them, life's ticking clocks.
Ebbing emotions, rising like foam,
The heart sways gently, we find our home.

In the swell of passion, we lose control,
Yet in the calm, we mend every hole.
Feelings collide like the currents strong,
In the ebb and flow, we find where we belong.

With every sunset, a chance to renew,
Riding the waves, we embrace what is true.
In the dance of the tides, our stories entwine,
Ebb and flow of feelings, forever divine.

Sailor of the Soul

In the quiet depths of the ocean's embrace,
A sailor navigates through time and space.
With dreams as sails, he seeks the unknown,
Mapping the stars, where the heart has flown.

Waves whisper secrets only he hears,
Guiding his journey through hopes and fears.
The compass spins, but he finds his way,
Charting the waters where shadows sway.

Through storms that threaten to capsize the boat,
He rides the tempest, on passion he'll float.
In calm reflections, the shores shine bright,
A sailor of the soul, in the heart's light.

Anchored in moments we cherish the most,
He carries our laughter, our love, and our ghost.
A voyage of spirit, he sails through the night,
Forever the sailor, our guiding light.

Harboring Thoughts

In the stillness of the night,
Whispers linger like shadows.
Dreams drift softly, out of sight,
Carried by the gentle meadows.

Beneath the moon's silver glow,
Wishes weave through the air.
Each secret the heavens know,
Cradled softly with care.

Fleeting moments lost in time,
Captured like a fleeting flame.
The echoes of a whispered rhyme,
Remind me of love's sweet name.

Every thought a gentle tide,
Washing over the jagged shore.
In this harbor, dreams abide,
Yearning for forevermore.

As dawn breaks with tender light,
Thoughts linger in morning's embrace.
With each breath, I find my height,
In the quiet, I find my place.

The Lapping of Quiet Remembrance

Gentle waves kiss the shore,
Softly whispering the past.
Memories like shells explore,
Carried on a breeze so fast.

Time slips through, a subtle thief,
Stealing hearts with every wave.
In the depths, I find my grief,
But also strength, the tide is brave.

Echoes dance upon the sand,
Telling tales of those long gone.
In this place, I understand,
Life continues—carried on.

The moon watches from above,
Guarding secrets of the night.
In the silence, there is love,
A beacon's glow, quiet light.

As the dawn begins to sing,
Memories fade with the mist.
But in the heart, echoes cling,
A gentle hug from what we've kissed.

Buoyant Sentiments

Floating high on the breeze,
Joyful whispers lift my soul.
Like a leaf among the trees,
I surrender to the whole.

Each thought, a feathered dream,
Soaring through the endless sky.
Radiant like a sunbeam,
With every breath, I learn to fly.

Laughter dances on the air,
Bright and free, it finds a home.
In this moment, without care,
I embrace the world to roam.

Every heartbeat sings a tune,
Melodies of sweet release.
Underneath the glowing moon,
In this stillness, I find peace.

As the stars begin to blink,
I let go of worries past.
With each heartbeat, I feel linked,
To the universe, vast and vast.

The Drift of Silent Contemplation

In quiet corners of the mind,
Thoughts drift like clouds on a breeze.
Seeking peace, I hope to find,
Moments wrapped in gentle ease.

A stillness wraps the evening hour,
As shadows stretch and softly sway.
In this place, I feel the power,
Of silence guiding me to stay.

With every sigh, the world slows down,
In the hush, I hear my heart.
Thoughts like leaves fall without a sound,
A tapestry of which I'm part.

Drifting in this tranquil sea,
I explore the depths within.
Each reflection beckons me,
To embrace the light I've been.

As the night lends its cool embrace,
I find solace in the dark.
In silent contemplation's grace,
I ignite my inner spark.

Whispering Depths

In shadows deep, the secrets flow,
A silent tide where dreams do go.
Echoes call from depths untold,
In murky waters, truths unfold.

Beneath the waves, my heart does sway,
A haunting chorus, night and day.
The whispers brush against my skin,
A dance of thoughts, where rifts begin.

In every wave, a tale is spun,
A journey shared, not just for one.
Through liquid realms, my spirit drifts,
Amongst the currents, my soul sifts.

A flicker bright, a moment's grace,
In the depths' hold, I find my place.
Suspended underneath the blue,
I hear the depths, I feel them too.

In quiet thought, I find my way,
Embraced by night, released by day.
The ocean's pulse, a gentle guide,
Through whispering depths, I glide, I ride.

The Ocean Within

In stillness lies a vast expanse,
A rush of tides in quiet dance.
Beneath the surface, currents swirl,
In every heartbeat, waves unfurl.

The ocean within, a mirror bright,
Reflecting dreams, both day and night.
With every breath, a silent storm,
In depths of hope, a soul reborn.

Emotions rise, like sand and sea,
A whirlpool's grip holds tight to me.
The ebb and flow, a rhythmic song,
Through storms of sorrow, I grow strong.

A lighthouse shines in darkest light,
Guiding my heart towards what's right.
The ocean within sings clear and true,
Whispers of wisdom, old yet new.

In every wave, a lesson learned,
The ocean's truth, forever yearned.
Through depths I wander, not alone,
In this vast sea, I've found my home.

Endless Surges of Sentiment

Like tides that ebb, then rush again,
My heart feels waves of joy and pain.
Endless surges, a dance of fate,
In ocean's arms, I contemplate.

With every rise, a memory calls,
A whispered song through water's walls.
The pull of love, the weight of fear,
In endless surges, I draw near.

Each crest a smile, each trough a sigh,
In currents strong, my hopes can fly.
The sea reflects what lies within,
A boundless realm where I begin.

The heart, like ocean, deep and vast,
Holds endless tales of future, past.
In fleeting moments, I collect,
Each wave's embrace, a wordless respect.

The rhythm holds me, fierce and true,
In endless surges, life anew.
With waves like breath, I rise, I fall,
In the ocean's grace, I've felt it all.

Castaway Musings

On shores of dreams, where time stands still,
A castaway sits, heart to fill.
Waves lap gently, secrets unfold,
Whispers of wonders, silent and bold.

With driftwood thoughts and shells of gold,
Stories linger, waiting to be told.
Each grain of sand holds echoes clear,
Of distant lands, of love sincere.

The horizon stretches, wide and great,
An endless quest, temptation's bait.
In solitude, my heart takes flight,
Through castaway musings, day and night.

The ocean's sigh, a lullaby sweet,
Guiding my soul with every beat.
In moonlit dreams, I wander free,
A castaway's heart, embracing the sea.

Each rising tide, a fresh embrace,
In this vast world, I've found my place.
With whispers soft, and tides that sway,
I cherish the night, the dawning day.

Coral Reefs of Recollection

Beneath the waves, colors gleam,
In tides of memory, we dream.
Life sways softly, a dance through time,
Where echoes whisper, hearts align.

Fragile corals hold our past,
In their embrace, we've found the vast.
Each creature swims with tales untold,
In azure depths, our dreams unfold.

Seashells gather stories rare,
Footprints fading, linger in air.
The gentle tide pulls us near,
A tranquil space, forgetting fear.

Upon these reefs, we drift and sway,
With every wave, let worries fray.
In vibrant hues, our spirits soar,
Recollection's depths, forevermore.

Underwater gardens, a secret keep,
In silence, memories gently seep.
Coral reefs, where time is sweet,
In watery realms, our hearts shall meet.

Sailboats of Solitude

Drifting softly on silent seas,
A lonely heart rides with the breeze.
Canvas wings catch whispers low,
In solitude, we chance to grow.

Stars above like dreams that glide,
On waves of thought, we gently ride.
Each drop of water, a moment shared,
In quietude, our souls prepared.

Horizon calls, an endless quest,
Seeking solace, we find our rest.
With every gust, the heart expands,
In solitude's embrace, life stands.

Anchored thoughts in twilight's glow,
The whispering winds, a soft echo.
Sailboats drift with gentle grace,
In silent seas, we find our place.

As dawn awakens with painted hues,
We set forth anew, chasing clues.
In solitude, the heart does sing,
Finding joy in what dreams bring.

Pearl of Possibility

Deep within the ocean's fold,
Lies a treasure, soft and bold.
A pearl shines bright, a wish untold,
In its layers, futures unfold.

Glistening dreams wrapped tight in grain,
Time and patience through joy and pain.
Each shimmer tells of light and dark,
A journey made from every spark.

Tides may shift, but hope remains,
In depths of struggle, growth sustains.
The pearl reveals what lies beneath,
In endless depths, we find belief.

Nature's gift, a symbol clear,
Of all that's possible, held near.
Emerging slowly, from hidden strife,
A pearl of possibility, our life.

So dive into the waves of chance,
Embrace the tides, let dreams enhance.
For in the depths, treasures await,
The pearl of hope, forever great.

Voyage of Inward Exploration

Set sail on thoughts, an inner quest,
Across the quiet seas, we rest.
Charting maps, where feelings flow,
Inward travel, a path to know.

Each wave a question, calm or fierce,
Within the depths, our truths pierce.
With compass turned toward fragile heart,
In stillness, fearless, we depart.

Islands of memory greet our gaze,
In shadows cast, the mind's strange maze.
Unraveling strands of tangled thought,
In the voyage, wisdom is sought.

Lessons emerge from silent tides,
Waves of insight, like gentle guides.
Through stormy realms, we navigate,
Embracing change, we resonate.

Inward exploration, a sacred art,
Finding solace within the heart.
In journeys deep, the spirit finds,
The richest treasures left behind.

Reflections in the Deep

Beneath the waves, a world unseen,
Mirrors of silence where thoughts convene.
Whispers of depths call out to the soul,
In the endless blue, I become whole.

Light dances softly, casting dreams wide,
With every shift, the tides coincide.
A shimmering surface, where secrets sleep,
In the quiet realm, I dare to leap.

Echoes of voices from the ocean floor,
Stories of wanderers, forevermore.
The pull of water, a gentle embrace,
In this sacred space, I find my place.

Time stands still in this liquid sphere,
Connecting my heart to all that I revere.
Each wave, a promise, each ripple, a sigh,
In the sea's vast cradle, I learn to fly.

A tapestry woven in colors so deep,
In the arms of the ocean, my dreams I keep.
Reflections in motion, both tender and grand,
In the depths of the sea, I take a stand.

Oceanic Reveries

Tides carry wishes on a soft, salty breeze,
   Gentle caresses that aim to please.
Each swell a whisper, each crest a song,
   In the ocean's arms, I feel I belong.

Dreams drift like seafoam, light and free,
   In the embrace of waves, a world to see.
Colors of twilight paint the horizon,
   As the sun dips low, my heart's a beacon.

Seagulls soar high, tracing paths in the air,
   Guiding lost souls with a timeless flare.
In the rhythm of currents, a tale unfolds,
Of ancient adventures, and treasures untold.

Footprints in sand, washed away with grace,
   Memories linger, but time leaves no trace.
In the tides' movement, I sense a dance,
   An oceanic reverie, a sweet romance.

As stars emerge, the night comes alive,
In the cool, soothing glow, I dive and strive.
   Infinite wonders await in the deep,
   In oceanic dreams, my heart will keep.

Currents of Curiosity

Whirling and twirling, the waters flow,
Each twist of fate teaches me to grow.
With open eyes, the depths invite,
Curiosity sparks under the moonlight.

Bubbles rise softly, secrets they share,
Dancing with shadows, floating on air.
Questions unravel like threads in the sea,
Each pull revealing more of me.

Underneath the surface, a pulse of life,
Creatures and colors cut through the strife.
In this vibrant chaos, I find my way,
Currents of wonder guide what I say.

Echoes of laughter play in the tide,
Curious spirits with nothing to hide.
Together we journey, exploring the blue,
Endless horizons offer something new.

With every wave that crashes and breaks,
I embrace the unknown, whatever it takes.
In the currents that move, I find my muse,
In the heart of the ocean, I never lose.

Sudden Swells of Inspiration

When the sea stirs, ideas take flight,
Sudden swells of inspiration ignite.
A single wave can change the course,
In the heart of chaos lies hidden force.

Splash of saltwater on sun-kissed skin,
Moments of clarity where thoughts begin.
Riding the swell, my spirit soars high,
In the pulse of the ocean, I learn to fly.

Every crest a canvas, each trough a chance,
To capture the essence in nature's dance.
Whirlwinds of thought crash like the tide,
In sudden surges, creativity won't hide.

Shadows and light weave a mystical thread,
Inspiration flows where the brave dare tread.
The ocean whispers secrets to those who seek,
In its ever-changing depths, I grow unique.

So I stand on the shore, arms stretched wide,
Embracing the waves, my heart open wide.
With sudden swells, my muse breaks free,
In the heart of the ocean, my spirit can be.

Cove of Contemplation

Quiet waves whisper low,
Underneath the soft skies.
Seagulls dance, a slow show,
Time drifts as the sun flies.

Shadows stretch, thoughts collide,
In the warmth of the sand.
The world outside can hide,
Here, peace takes a firm stand.

Shells gather stories near,
Each one holds a small tale.
Footprints fade without fear,
As gentle tides prevail.

The sunset paints the sea,
Blushing hues of deep gold.
In this serene reprieve,
Heart's secrets are retold.

Breath of salt lingers sweet,
With dusk's calming refrain.
In the night, dreams compete,
In the cove, thoughts remain.

Compass of Dreams

Starlit skies call my name,
Guiding wishes set free.
Each twinkle holds a flame,
A map meant just for me.

Winds whisper soft secrets,
Across the darkened sea.
In silence, no regrets,
Just longing to be free.

The north star shines so bright,
Leading ships through the night.
With every wave's embrace,
I find my destined place.

Horizons stretch afar,
A promise yet untold.
Each dream a shining star,
In skies of blue and gold.

Heartbeats in sync with tides,
I chase the breaking dawn.
With hope my spirit rides,
On dreams that linger on.

Islands of Echoes

Whispers in the breeze play,
Echoes of tales once shared.
Each wave holds a soft sway,
Moments cherished, declared.

Lighthouses guard the night,
Guiding souls lost at sea.
Voices rise, a soft light,
In the heart's memory.

Islands stand tall and proud,
Wrapped in mist's gentle veil.
Each voice, a ghostly crowd,
Tales of joy, love, and ail.

Footprints wash with the waves,
Leaving traces in sand.
Among the quiet graves,
Whispers still understand.

Time dances in shadow,
With every echoing sigh.
Bringing forth what we sow,
In the tides, dreams won't die.

Fluent in the Language of the Ocean

The ocean speaks in waves,
A language soft and clear.
Each crest holds the souls' braves,
In rhythms that draw near.

Salt and spray meld with air,
Whispers flowing like streams.
The currents softly share,
Secrets woven in dreams.

I listen to the tide,
With every pulse it sways.
It holds the world inside,
In its eternal plays.

Footfalls blend with the sea,
As footprints fade away.
In this dance, I am free,
Lost in the ocean's sway.

Moonlight guides my way home,
In the night's gentle arms.
Wherever I may roam,
The ocean's sound disarms.

Voyage of the Unfathomable

Upon the seas of azure vast,
We sail through shadows, veins of past.
Mysteries whisper in the breeze,
Guiding our hearts with gentle ease.

Stars ignite in the velvet night,
Navigating dreams, we discover light.
With every wave, our spirits soar,
The unknown shores beckon us more.

Harbors hidden, secrets unfold,
Tales of sailors, brave and bold.
In silence, we hear the ocean's call,
An endless journey, forever enthrall.

Each gleaming wave, a story untold,
Choices and chances, treasures we hold.
With courage found in the tempest's roar,
We chart a course to distant shore.

In depths profound, our souls will roam,
In the endless blue, we've found our home.
Together we sail through the night and day,
In this voyage of life, forever we stay.

Waves of Reflection

Whispers upon the gentle tide,
Mirror of dreams where thoughts confide.
Each ripple speaks of hidden fears,
In silence, we confront our tears.

The ocean's edge holds secrets deep,
Memories stored, a treasure to keep.
As surf embraces the sandy shore,
We seek the answers, forevermore.

Time drifts on like a feathered breeze,
Carrying echoes of distant seas.
In twilight's glow, the water gleams,
Reflecting all of our wildest dreams.

With every crash, our voices join,
The symphony sung in the ocean's coin.
A dance of shadows, light, and sound,
In waters vast, our truths are found.

In stillness, we gaze at the vast expanse,
Learning to embrace our fate's sweet dance.
Every wave a lesson, every tide a chance,
In the rhythms of life, we find our stance.

Deep Currents of the Mind

Beneath the surface, thoughts flow fast,
In currents dark, our shadows cast.
The depths are vast, we dare to dive,
Exploring realms where dreams survive.

With every swell, new ideas rise,
A spiral dance beneath the skies.
In hidden caves, our fears reside,
Yet hope emerges like the morning tide.

The mind is ocean, wild and deep,
In it, the secrets we can keep.
Through winding tunnels, bright and bleak,
The quest for truth is what we seek.

Diving deeper, we face our fears,
The depths reveal both joys and tears.
Through inner storms and calms sublime,
We navigate the sands of time.

In every thought, a wave of change,
In every choice, a path rearranged.
With courage born from deep within,
We sail the currents where life begins.

Driftwood Dreams

On shores where time begins to sleep,
Driftwood whispers secrets it keeps.
Each weathered piece tells tales of yore,
As nature weaves wonders on the floor.

Found at dusk, as shadows creep,
The dreams we drift with, wild and deep.
Gone are the burdens of yesterday,
In wooden fragments, we find our way.

Like boats abandoned, waiting still,
Among the sands, we seek our will.
Each splinter speaks of journeys past,
Reminding us that nothing lasts.

The tide returns with memories bare,
As driftwood carries wishes, rare.
With every wave that breaks anew,
We gather dreams in shades of blue.

In twilight's glow, we build anew,
Crafting life from pieces true.
Among the driftwood, hope aligns,
In dreams adrift, our future shines.